birth of the uncool

birth of the uncool

POEMS BY

Madeline Walker

DEMETER

DEMETER PRESS, BRADFORD, ONTARIO

Canada Council for the Arts **Conseil des Arts du Canada**

The publisher gratefully acknowledges the support of the Canada Council for the Arts for its publishing program.

Demeter Press
c/o Motherhood Initiative for Research and
Community Involvement (MIRCI)
140 Holland St. West, P.O. 13022
Bradford, ON, L3Z 2Y5
Telephone: 905.775.9089
Email: info@demeterpress.org
Website: www.demeterpress.org

Demeter Press logo based on the sculpture, "Demeter" by Maria-Luise Bodirsky <www.keramik-atelier.bodirsky.de>

Front cover artwork: Michael Carpenter

Library and Archives Canada Cataloguing in Publication

Walker, Madeline, 1958–, author
Birth of the uncool : poems / by Madeline Walker.

ISBN 978-1-927335-37-6 (pbk.)

I. Title.

PS8645.A462B57 2014 C811'.6 C2014-901973-4

Printed and Bound in Canada

This book is dedicated to my parents,
Ken and Virginia, for making life
and to Michael, for making life wonderful.

Contents

V. Birth of the Uncool

I. Recovery

If the only prayer you ever say in your entire life is thank you,
that will be enough.

—Meister Eckhart

My Ariadne

Part I

-1-

I sleep on the ponderous foot of Ariadne,
my world.
I doze in her long stride, she decides
how to walk the labyrinth today.

The Minotaur is a metaphor.
Sub-clinical anxiety and ever-present dread are
the human condition.

My Ariadne punts out dread each morning
with a double kick: gratitude and meditation.

She never noticed Theseus—
Some guy in her peripheral vision.

"But that's ridiculous! It's not the same myth, then!"

She told me she is here to lead me
through this life.

Thank you,
thank you, my Ariadne.

- 2 -

Yes, my Ariadne is married to
Dionysius.

It's not that he took pity
on her when Theseus
deserted her. No, not at all.
She was never deserted,
only desserted by Dio—her sweet tooth is legendary.

Another thing,
She didn't reform Dio—
Far from it.
He decided to quit booze
all by himself—before he met her.

"Dionysis without wine? Nonsense."

They are soberly happy
together.

- 3 -

Sometimes
I ride on her hand
through space and time.
Her palm is rough,
criss-crossed deep
with woe and joy.

I curl there, like a cat
and feel lulled by her
movement,
feel safe doing her will.

Part II

- 4 -

Wake up! You must not
leave everything to mythic
narrative, to the will of a
goddess!

Are you lazy? Passive?
Null?

No. I recreated her after
Nietzsche, after Chirico.
I made her all mine.
That—*that*—requires
the courage
of the innocent child.

- 5 –

Chirico spent six decades obsessed
with the Ariadne abandoned by
Theseus on the
Island of Naxos.

He painted, sculpted, drew,
and wrote about a woman forsaken,
a woman paralyzed, a woman frozen in marble,
alone.

My Ariadne was never discarded.
She never even noticed Theseus.
My Ariadne claims the labyrinth,
strides through this open-air maze daily.

Hummingbirds feed from her
mouth; muscles ripple in her
dark thigh; her hair is lit by
purple glow; her smile is caught
by the sun and mirrored across
the world.

- 6 –

Nietzsche's Ariadne was tortured,
demented by pain, by love.
Not so mine.

I ride on her back or her foot, in her
pocket or her palm, depending on the
hour, the weather.

Today we are gliding across
high terrain, winds whip her hair
lovingly, playfully.
Shards of rock
fall in love with her tough and
shapely feet.

Part III

– 7 –

The weight of old myth
lays heavy on the present
presses up through time,
insists, berates.
Men belaboring
the thread, the sorrow,

and Ariadne's acquiescence.

The old Greek and Roman names are
roots cracking the earth,
threatening to crush light language.

But what's this?
The tiny frame of a miniature
woman stretched out to her
full five inches
back arched, incorrigible,
feet planted on palm

"NON SERVIAM"
she yells full-throated

and Ariadne stops,
looks down with love-
glazed eyes. "I know,
my darling, I know."

And we are off again.

- 8 -

There is no thread to follow,
no charted way.
Ariadne follows hunches,
intuition, the universe's
whisper.

The thread—with its beginning,
its end—Ariadne giving it, Theseus following it…
is another version,
Not ours.

At times our way is elliptical, difficult,
other times direct and easy.
Ariadne rests her feet often
and invites visions of what her next step
might be.

Remember, there is no beast
to conquer or escape.
There is only Dio to meet for coffee
at three. Sweet anticipation!

- 9 -

"Ariadne without Theseus
can't possibly still be Ariadne.
What are you thinking?"

Angela Carter morphed
Perrault's Bluebeard into
a tale of woman's power to reform.
She transformed the bloody chamber
into a school for blind children.

James Joyce made the great mythical
wanderer Ulysses
into a fattish Jewish man and described
his relish for urine-scented kidneys,
his pleasure in the outhouse.

Take Theseus
and demote him to tailor pulling threads.
Elevate my goddess to her deserved height,
pull the power from rock, sky, ocean,
invest her fleshy body
with that strength.

Pop me into the pocket of her
rough purple shift.
Give her leather sandals today
and springy dark hair—masses of it.
Make the world her labyrinth
and let her breathe love.

Now, *that's* my Ariadne.

Storm

That dream storm last night
had me drunk, late for something important
my wallet was stolen, or the purse,
the papers were out of order
somebody was disappointed in me
"Shame, shame on you"
my face was aflame and it felt like fever

The past is a glowering sky sometimes
pushing down on me
like humidity does on sultry August days
the thunder is brewing out there
and the clouds turn gassy green on their
bellies

Cloudburst dreams
expel old hurts and fancies,
old remnants of addiction
betrayals, burns, guile and guilt

Cleanse me, dreams, of the past
flatten me: roll humiliation
from out my finger tips...let the needle points of
cold, sharp water drive memories
from my pores

let me wake to this present—clean, rested.
My mind light and white and bare as a hospital room
the blue pill having mown the jungle
and like a hand across the rainy sky
cleared the slate for sun.
The rain evaporates—
vapour rises from white tile.

Local sources

Here is the source of
Shame:
Down at the brown root
of decomposition we are all alike
yet the split self
imagines we should be different,
more polished and clean,
less heavy matter, more white light.

Here is the source of
Guilt:
Down at the pink root you let
desire pull you out of your
rational mind, and the split
self hates you for following
that fucking pulse. Will you
ever forgive?

Here is the source of
Hate:
Down in the gut the bile
forms jagged green stones that
you throw at your enemies—
Construct your wall
and start pelting.

Here is the source of
Love:
Up in the vermilion chamber
a glossy red starts to
flow. Like hot lava it bubbles
over, eating your shame,
your guilt,
your hate,
healing the split self.

Recovery means

When I was young,
women like me were an
embarrassment.
Exposing their jiggly upper arms,
showing their cracks and their boulders,
leaking from sweet, runny centers,
hugging crying sweating feeling laughing loud,
taking up space in the world.

Now I've grown into one of those women.

Recovery means embracing what
was shunned, gathering what was
scattered, honouring the
molten heart, taking up space, not
apologizing for being human, fallible, female,
loving intensely, speaking truth,
embarrassing young folks.

Feed your demon

Blue demon guilt
your tensile strength,
female, unrelenting,
            rails against me.

Sinewed arm of
barbed tendon presses
hard against my soft
flesh.   Your face

is one blue contortion,
shivering with ague,
purple valleys
                    sink your eyes.

Eyes that spit black seeds at me;
you throw back all my
misdeeds, spanning
                    centuries.

Repulsive, your pudendum:
convex, hard, Boschian.
                    Who are your children?

Oh, are you *my* mother then?
I never realized. Then
where is your mother-love?

Raging blue claws
incise my shoulders
tattoo me with
guilt's deep pigment.

Feel me falling away,
blue mother, under your
grip, dissolving to nectar.

Take me into your cave-mouth
Take me under your sharp tongue
I will feed you, sweeten your blue
core to indigo, make you my ally.

The Dr. Seuss Challenge

I have trouble remembering that you are yourself
Though there's books all about it up there on the shelf
You are you, I am I, and though I care very much
It's important I stay out of your adult stuff

You see co-dependence is a strange little dance
makes my caretaker self enter caretaking trance
I worry 'til all of my worry slots fill
then start building YOUR life in my life-making mill

The hardest of lessons is to sit on my hands
keep my tongue in my mouth, tend to Madeline lands
Your lands, son, are yours, with your own skies above
I'll keep to my acreage, just sending out love.

*Imitate the rhythm and rhyme scheme of a
Dr. Seuss poem (try it)

I have heard there are troubles of more than one kind.
Some come from ahead and some come from behind.
But I've bought a big bat. I'm all ready you see.
Now my troubles are going to have troubles with me!

from Dr. Seuss's *I Had Trouble Getting to Solla Sollew* (1965)

Bleak trail

bleak trail you've gouged here

scant sun through the crabbed trees

you're wasting the miles, you know.

monotonous trail

aren't you tired yet

of the same landscape,

the same dark sky every day,

the same trees reaching out and

grabbing you, pulling you down in the mud

again and again?

There is an

alternate path over there.

Many travellers on the

brighter road have yelled, waved prayer

flags, and hooted.

But your head stays down.

For a long time, I travelled with

you, urging you to

switch paths. Recently

I detoured to the bright way

to save my life.

I used to catch a glimpse

of you through crabbed trees

struggling over the ruts,

but I hated to watch you suffer. So

I have gone on ahead. Forgive me.

Keep

Housekeeping
all that mess got
in the way of
finding home.
In the clearing,
here's ground for the
new idea, new love.

Voicekeeping
trying too hard to
sound throaty, cool,
to belt out the
blues, leaves a voice
reedy, thin. Un-
cover the clear high
bell of the child's voice
that you once wanted
to lose under the
old tyranny of nice.

Soulkeeping
blunt atheism
concussed
your soul—the
one you thought
didn't exist—and
then, just in time,

you recovered the
waif and cradled her,
taught her
trust, taught her
faith.

retain possession
of your house, your
voice, your soul.
Keep them.

Leaf people

dry brown leaf people scud toward me
on a low wind
Hello! hello there! they cry
We're almost done. The next rain will
paste us into mud. Enjoy us now.
Be present.
Listen to our scratchy glide
experience the crunch your boot makes
loving us.
You are alive, alive!
Now, the time is now!

Out of caves into the light

Roll under the tablecloth little boy
it's safe under there
out here it's bicker, slam, stomp, yell

Suck your thumb
they cannot hear you weep

. . .

Roll under the trembling green and silver
curtain of the weeping willow

Suck your joint, boy
let smoke scour your aching
throat hold back the tears.

. . .

Some time ago you left the
darkness of caves, entered light.
You raked fear, denial
in a heap with scrappy leaves,
watched them burn to ash.

Out of all caves now, man,
suck air, suck the marrowed
savory of life.

Epistemology check

This thin sheet of plasterboard knowledge
covers a chasm of ignorance,
deep and wide.

I am still asking, in late middle age, the child's questions:
Is there a god?
What is life's purpose?
Why is the sky blue?

Instead of pretending the plasterboard will hold
into old age
I'll dismantle it now
Belay a running rope and
Get some sturdy climbing boots

I'm going down.

Third step, a villanelle

"Turn it over" is the mantra of my days
each stumble has me pivoting toward you
My mind resists and yet my heart obeys

I know it's more than just a phase
Until I die, this is what I'll do
"Turn it over" is the mantra of my days

My crazy will still wants her crazy ways
"Turn it over"? Higher power who?
My mind resists and yet my heart obeys

A curious calm, after numerous delays
My will surrenders, I feel a little blue
"Turn it over" is the mantra of my days

Then warmth creeps in like sun's slant rays
serene and kind—why, this is new!
My mind resists and yet my heart obeys

Here's peace that settles down and stays
Here's something deep, and warm, and true
"Turn it over" is the mantra of my days
My mind resists and yet my heart obeys

II. Youth

Nostalgia is only amnesia turned around.

—Adrienne Rich

The Stag

for Elizabeth Bishop

I faced a stag
in the darkening light,
felt his animal breath
warm, familiar
looked into his glassy
dispassionate eye
felt a whoosh of joy
to share the earth.

There was a moment of
recognition. How did
you raise forty points
on urban marigolds?
I wanted to ask, and wanted
him to answer, plunging us from
Oak Bay to Narnia

I could be Susan,
Archeress, older sister
for once—surefooted,
gentle, strong,
doubtful at first, but
then devoted to Aslan for
a time.

Stag, turn white and take me there,
let me blow danger with my
magic horn before I get
beguiled by the material world.

But oh! suddenly
the fling of mind back to body,
yours— pivot of bone branches,
smooth quivering hide,
and mine—sagging on two legs

in this sad
outlandish standoff.
Sad because you may
be culled untimely from
our shared earth.

Schoolgirl

yearning

playing on the girls' side of the
schoolyard and longing, even in
kindergarten, for boys—
admiring their reckless play from afar
loving their bodies' swarm
like flesh on the bones of the jungle gym,
skin-to-skin jostling,
bronze shouts clanging the air.
On our side girls
stood skirted in clots whispering
tales, our jungle gym
a set of dead bones.

pride

Soon I understand
I am smart and good. While the
bad boys get spanked by Mrs.
Howden, I win the spelling quiz,
get to clean the erasers, come
home with the badge of chalk
dust on my kilt. Oh knocky-
kneed chatty school girl I
was! I wish I could hug

her now in her then unself-
conscious uncool glory
because soon it will wither

fear

fear that I wasn't doing it
right I didn't look right nobody
liked me fear I was silly, dumb,
ugly, fat, too smart, uncool, wrong clothes
fear somebody would intuit
I was not solid but hollow, and
be disappointed like at Easter
when you thought the bunny
was chocolate all the way through
only to have the thin casing melt
in your hands, revealing a brown cavity

envy

my supercool sister wore a mini
as tiny as a hankie and school
boys thronged her,
soaking up her body heat
hanging on her flirty words.
I was always slightly off
kilter, off rhythm, not
getting the obscure
syncopation of beguilement
still I yearned for male attention,
just as I did in kindergarten, with
bruised knees, gazing at the
boys' side, thirsty

yearning

In grad school the same hot pride, fear,
and envy flooded my
viscera. Feel
pride pulse (I'm smart)
fear ache
(they'll find out I'm not so smart)
envy grate (I wish I were as smart
as she is)

The boys are now
professors heating up the jungle
gym with their jostling, raucous cries of
knowledge, and again, I am
entranced, thirsty, yearning,
a schoolgirl at the edge of
the schoolyard, hanging on
their alloyed words.

Looking a gift horse in the mouth

Rough wooden limbs, crude
painted faces. Maid Marian had
a mop of red hair, a red gown,
Robin Hood a brutish chin,
a cheap green felt hat.
Why marionettes, grandmother?

Puppets pulled lifeless
from long boxes.
Dull heaps for me to animate.

Soon I had seven of the damn
things and I was only seven.
They hung from special hooks
in my bedroom, little
corpses dangling in the
moonlight, infiltrating
my dreams.

I toyed with them,
desultorily,
invited friends over to
put on a puppet show.
But there was something
obscene in the leery wooden
faces and twitching bodies.

I felt so clumsy pulling their
strings.

Before long the tangles
started.
This, and then the next, and the next puppet
were tied up, unusable, their bodies
wrapped in webs of black.
I don't know how it happened.
I sat cross-legged on the floor,
ashamed, crying,
unable to pick apart
the hard math of string with
my small fingers.

Oh grandmother, why not
music boxes or dolls like
you gave my sisters?
Why is mine the burden
of unraveling these
strings, over, and over,
like some entry-level Sisyphus?

Daisy

"Every childhood's conflictual experiences remain
hidden and locked in darkness, and the key to our
understanding of the life that follows is
hidden away with them."
Alice Miller

A persistent dream from
early years: I burrowed through
a dark tunnel just big enough for
my lithe body. It was
a long scary time of clawing and scrambling
through dirt.
But finally I came up into the day and
a big daisy—such a cartoonish flower—
was handed to me.
I sat on green grass at the mouth of the hole,
crosslegged, light, my bones like a bird's, holding a large
white-petalled, yolk-centred flower that seems now like the repository
of all happiness!
And all of the hard painful scary work
of traversing that tunnel was gone (poof)
in one moment.

There are so many births, so many forgettings.
We endure our dark tunnels,
claw through depression.
Then we rise up and are handed happiness in a flower.
I like to think the dark canal of death
is followed by a daisy, too.

Coming of age in Toronto

Yonge Street Mall* is the place to be
Late afternoon presses into muggy evening
Pavements throng. Trees in concrete boxes have
been trucked into mid-town for this experiment; the air is festive.
Women in miniskirts laugh and lick ice cream cones.
Cigarette smoke floats into the black sky and
bar doors open, music pounds the night.

Barefoot, I walk the Yonge Street Mall with
my sister with flower-painted cheeks through saliva and dirt and over
cigarette butts and spilled drinks, melting ice cream, the
fray of our elephant bellbottoms scuffing dirty pavement.
We come home so filthy, the dirt worked so deeply
into our cracked soles we don't come clean for days. And then we
do it again.
My mother scolds us,
but by then
we are uncontrollable.

I am dressed in a nylon white uniform,
my long brown hair pulled back in a pony tail.
I make $2.75 an hour for scooping ice cream and showing my
body to strangers: "I can see right through that dress,
you know" one guy says, winking, as he takes his rum 'n raisin
single scoop
from my hand.

My knuckles scrape against the sides of the plastic tub
as I dig deep into frozen chocolate, hand cold, raw, sticky,
coated in melting brown. Sometimes the scoops slide off the
Styrofoam-like cones and people want their money back.
A little boy cries over his fallen scoop dissolving on the street.

"Press down hard" says my coworker Milt. We do the same work,
but for every hour he is paid one dollar more.

I bend and scoop right next to the plate glass window
We are lit up hard those hot summer nights,
harsh fluorescents over the 24 flavors.
My feet and legs cramp from standing, my scraped and freezing
hands burn.
My heart is hard packed
down in the core, flash frozen at the point of feeling,
held at cryogenic temps.
Ochre sadness, brown despair, white fear. When they thaw, if they thaw,
will it be very painful, like chilblained hands warmed over the fire?

Men and boys look at me through the window.
They can see my bra and panties through the sheer material. I feel
eyes on
me as I bend and scoop, bend and scoop. The boss, a Columbian
drug dealer
in sunglasses, wants me to work the window spot.
My new breasts ache as I lean into the metal edge of the

ice cream cooler. My thighs and hips are thickening into woman.

Next summer the Mall is back.
I take a dozen pink Gravol because somebody
said it would get you really high for cheap.
I walk the Mall alone in the high blaze of July
All of the buildings and people are dis-located in my
eye, floating, dancing, sinking, heavy. Sounds come at me
in sheets of slow gurgle. The sky is screaming
blue. I lurch and vomit. People make a wide circle around
the stink and mess, leery of this crazy-high teenage girl with long stringy hair,
tattered jeans, feelings hard-packed-deep.

* * *

That autumn I covet a bolt of cornflower blue viyella. That
otherworldly blue, that smooth cloth, held the promise of some better place.
While my mother chooses fabric for curtains,
I lean my face against the soft nap and imagine cutting and sewing
Simplicity 5339, a high-necked ruffle-bottomed nightgown. Surely
that nightie could return me to girlhood, to innocence.

*For three years in the early 1970's Toronto's Yonge Street—between Gerrard and Richmond—was closed at various times during the summer, up to eleven weeks at one time. The experiment was intended to bring more pedestrians into the downtown core.

Bell bottom blues

Bell bottom blues was the song she sang
to lure the guitarist in
basement jam sessions, so cliché,
she rasps her seventeen-year old
voice to cigarette sexy, catching
the eye of Nils on
his Stratocaster, his remote Neanderthal skull
decorated with long straw.

"If I could choose a place
to die it would be in your arms"

One night they
fall asleep sodden drunk in
one another's arms, candles
burning, wake choking
on smoke, flames eating the mattress.
He leaps from the balcony,
long bare body
a white arc as he soars briefly
in pale light.
Chagrined, heel cracked, he limps
bare-assed along College Street.

Alone and naked on the balcony,
she calls for anybody's help as
smoke pours from the door behind her

Rescued by a firefighter on
a ladder who
throws a thick blanket 'round her
smudged breasts,
she tastes the smoke
in her mouth for weeks.

Broad back of life

Day comes blooming
up, thick clouds,
indifferent to people and
their lives.
Day is day, just useless,
just what it is:
making weather,
blowing fog, lifting veils,
passing time, nothing
to lose or to gain,
leaving itself alone.

A little girl chews her hair
into a wet tail
How many homophones
can she find by tomorrow?
reign rain/ pare pair
Dane deign/ fair fare
Her father worries
about her, she worries
about him, worries multiply.

She masticates the hair tail,
a worry knot grows in her tum
the babysitter said a hair ball
was growing in there,
getting bigger and bigger.

Little girl, instead of chasing
homophones, why don't you
learn to ride life?
Relax your moving mouth
and squinched eyes, let your body
melt, open up to the great flawed
masterpiece of the useless
day—making weather pushing
clouds passing time.

Imagine you can ride easy on the
broad back of life.

Paradise lost

I slept off another drunk
and woke to see boots

walking by, the gray November
day, the dirty basement window.

I was unspoiled once, and open, like
calendula's orange splendor at noon.

Then, I shut down: Not by one event,
(Eve's serpent), not by one great Fall,

but by many little stumbles, stains,
tiny losses, small shames. I bottomed out.

. . .

One day in December 1976
I listened to Milton's lines, book nine,
spoken in my professor's

baritone, that magnificent
story of the Fall of Man.

"their minds
How darkened; innocence, that as a veil
Had shadowed them from knowing ill, was gone"

I sat in the gloom of the lecture hall
smashed by life, shame burning
my wick. Unbelievably, I felt the Fall,
like hurtling rock, like a ripping veil,
the center dropping out of everything.

Nostalgia loves a story: once
Heinemann stood proud, upright in
my radiant room. Cats sunbathed,
there were piano lessons, ballet classes,
pink tights, clean windows like cathedrals
up high, unblotted open days
dancing by like shadows on the
frangible screen of innocence.

Motherlode

In a clan of ginger, your dark crown pulled the eye.
Beautiful ungainly schwartz
learned to pick peaches at 6,
to drive a car at 12.
You were a barefoot child,
smoldering into life.

Your seed sprang from
hard dry loins of dustbowl farms,
you blossomed dark to light,
turned burlap sacks to rickracked frocks,
pushed hard against poverty,
ate books, ached for knowledge,
opened your scarred scared heart to love.

Passionate proud creature, you live
inside me, your pepper cutting
through my honey, brave unexpected heat
sears the surprised and happy tongue.

III. Motherhood

My role is important, but not unique, and I don't expect to see it in lights.

—Anonymous

As was your plan

We didn't realize
you had plans
for those huge feet
those massive hands

that at your birth
so surprised me
size disproportioned
to your infancy

The plan unpacks:
large hands hold and
shake metal cans
steel peas clack

Your face ecstatic in the flow
In the secret glow
Of the paint dance
The stalk of your long
body in ssssst trance

While other kids gave homemade
cards you painted MOM a metre
high behind Safeway (thanks)

You leap about, make jewelled faces,
letters everywhere that vanish,

without traces, your marks
ephemeral as your sadness,
joy nudges away madness and
you paint again,

As was your plan.

MOTHER to mother

My ex-husband has a car full of our sons and he and his current wife
are driving to Costco for food
they pick me up on the side of the road
where I am looking over a fenced field of babies.
In the back seat there is a quiet freckled son I had forgotten about,
or didn't know I had,
named Sandy.
I try to make it up to him—"I'll take you to a movie,
but not this Sunday, because it's father's day," I say.
Sandy is remote; he doesn't really know me.

They drop me off on the side of the road and I
negotiate two buses home.

My curriculum vitae included, at the top,
MOTHER.
When I got home I
replaced it with mother in the list of other roles
(writer, wife, teacher, mother).

I wasn't perfect. I neglected you sometimes.
I didn't remember about Sandy.

Cupcake

Decorate your own cupcake!
Big bowls of soft
butter icing—hot pink, sky blue,
mint green, daffodil yellow—
liquefy under molten sun.
Two dozen chocolate cupcakes
on a tray, brown soldiers
in white wrappers.

Choice of toppings—gummi bears congeal
in one bowl, chocolate chips melt
in another. Sprinkles of all colors
and shapes.

Sun bakes the grass to straw.

Ten whooping boys scoop
icing dollops onto cupcakes.
Crush of boy energy, wiry bodies
masticate, spit, yell, throw,
leap, jostle, push, shriek.
Skinny panting chests streaked
with war paint frosting.

One small boy at the
margins architects
his cupcake with

great care.
Blue icing built into
cloud formations, sprinkled
with silver stars, too beautiful to eat.

You are still blessed.
You shut out the crash of the world and
rest serene in the
friendly geometry of your mind.

Big rock candy mountain

There was always some
new scheme, a fresh
game, a ripe moment
to rise up in the world
to get something for nothing

But here we are huddled
around a small electric
heater so Dad can sleep
(the furnace makes too much
noise clanking its
ancient machinery)

When we are always
looking around the bend

When we are always
counting on the next
big payoff, the sweet
win, the harvest

We are never actually here
harvesting this moment:
watching babies grow,
ladling hot soup,
feeling the wind rush in the
door to kiss our faces,
right here, right now

Genealogy

I know the gene bequeathed
is not my fault.
I ask forgiveness anyway.

Scientists announced
they'd almost isolated the little fucker in their
slick white labs. If only I could
have swiped out that gene,
surreptitiously, from the soup
that made you, spliced in
something else—an extra love gene
perhaps.

But then, what loss? What might
we have missed? Your smoky
intensity, blue depths, brooding
passions? Your courage to climb out of the
tar pit? The wisdom that comes of suffering?

Vacation on the farm

Here the scudding clouds fly
over the wide fields,
over the tree fort,
over the leaning barn.
Here's adventure for
a small boy visiting

his grandfather's farm.
Here is the huge horse called,
jokingly, Poco. Evan is scared
of the tall legs and switch tail
but he loves to hold an apple
to horse lips curling back over

huge yellow teeth. Poco's
resplendent tongue removes the fruit
gently. Here are white
swans on brown glass.
His grandfather taught
him to be quiet, to be still

as they glide undisturbed
like fairy tale creatures.
Here is the fowl pen, where

Evan loves to watch
the chickens clucking over
their grain, heads dipping
under the coxcomb rooster.

One morning the air
tastes of metal. Thirty seven
headless hens,
blood on the fence,
feathered bodies old rags.
My father wishes he could hide
death from his grandson,
as Evan stares through the
hole torn in the
slats and begins to cry.

Light the way

You waney moon
87 percent visible,
gibbous, glowing,
light the way for our
children out there

on beaches drinking
purloined beer
and mickeys booted
by older sisters,
brothers

perching narrow
buttocks on driftwood
and lighting one
cigarette off the glowing
end of the other

kissing deeply, inexpertly
with all the fervour
of adolescent desire
I want you I need you

vomiting in sand and
covering it like a cat
covers her scat. Careening
drunkenly, shouting,

loving-hating freedom,
life

fumbling with condoms,
sucking on joints, warming
cold hands over the meagre
fire. And then the looming

figures stride toward them
with flashlight beams
splitting their warm bodies
ok ok, time to go home
now kids, break it up now

and perhaps 20 minutes
later you see your
slim daughter slide
up the back stairs,
mascara running,
unsteady on her feet
a wan smile flashed
at you, inscrutable.

Youngest learns to ride a bike

To watch your youngest child
learn to ride a bike is to let go the seat,
release the boy to gravity.
"Are you still holding?" he cries
"No" and he cascades
fierce, joyous, flying
cross the pavement
"I'm riding, I can ride a bike!"

You sit now, easing sore back
against a tree, hands idle hanging low,
etched with flight paths of children
that have ventured forth.
Now your last charts his
ever widening circles
pumping, wobbly, coursing with glee.

And you, peripheral, remember
Le Conte School yard, Berkeley.
Your young father runs beside you,
glasses clunk against his beaky nose.
"Are you still holding?" you yell,
Your hair whipping back, the sky aching blue
"No" he laughs and you are flying
too.

Young noble

Your broad brow is a bridge from your hair to your
face—oh what a noble
face. Nobility cultivated,
not inherited.

Your hair is now negligible.
Your girl sheared it like Delilah
Samson, but only ego fell away with
your brown locks, not strength.

Your noble face again, in repose,
so still I could have sworn you were
struck dumb but the zing of
kinesis in your temple shows
the living cells working.

Now we break bread
together. You carefully dissect
the fish, the greens, and quietly
nourish your tall strong body.

More and more, silence is an
option. We sit companionably
in the lamplight reading.

Eldest son

They said you looked like an old man when you were born
wizened, burdened by some ancient wisdom.
And it was a hard birth.
Yearned for, but difficult in coming.
All at once you wore us out, touched us, shook us up
we laughed and cried at your red beginning.

Instead of clinging close
you pulled away from us.
At eight months old
walking too soon on tiny perfect feet
you staggered boldly into the world
never to look back.

I loved you then with a sometimes sad ferocity.
There was headiness in watching you, first born,
careening unafraid into the world
Precocious and darkly beautiful.
But I was scared by your unusualness,
scared by your adamantine will.

You careened into darkness,
were blindsided by hard
walls, you were tumbled by life.

Then you came through yesterday,
out of passive voice, still
trailing the tattered mantle
of your pain, yet smiling
ruefully, unbelievably loving,
ready for more.

IV. Coming Home

We must laugh and we must sing,
We are blest by everything,
Everything we look upon is blest.
—W. B. Yeats, "A Dialogue of Self and Soul"

Around the house:
A week of domestic sedokas

* Monday *

butter gets ready
—mud-soft in a tiny dish—
for spreading on a toast snack

peach jam on the knife
hovers over the brown toast
waiting to marry butter

* Tuesday *

I change the bed sheets
your black sock is revealed there
between crumpled red linen

What good is a sock
without a foot? Or a mate?
I tuck it in your drawer

* Wednesday *

I hear the subtle
crunch of cat kibble against
Andy's teeth, and then silence

After a moment,
the lup lup lup lup lup lup
of Andy drinking water

* Thursday *

Nothing happening.
Sun hits the edge of the couch
and travels slowly across

Refrigerator murmurs
A dust mote drifts through the air,
Nothing happening today

* Friday *

Mail thunks on hall floor
Together, cats raise their heads
in mild interest at the noise

Listen to the steps
of the letter carrier
grow fainter. Lay down your heads

* Saturday *

We failed to dead head
the calendula, and now
they'll take the garden

Hordes of orange blossom
are expected next summer
Will we still be here?

* Sunday *

Black grounds in the sink
coffee cup on the counter
traces of Sunday morning

We work parallel
I hear your pencil moving
when my sewing machine stops

Marriages past and present

Residue of other marriages
shows up from time to time
—sticky snail trails, not quite dried
into lacquer.

There is the handwriting
on the old spice jars:
time capsules from the 1990s.

That ex-wife's loopy script
sure, bold: Dried Basil
Why write "dried"
when it's bloody obvious?

Most of the other traces are
beautiful, benign. The children, for
instance. The blocky pot, the watercolour
by the first wife, a potter, an artist.

Those bodies before her—what
did their nipples taste like? how
did their sweat smell? Did they laugh
at his jokes?

Fed elixer ("I've never
loved like this before"), she
settles down, replaces the
spice jars, admires the children.

Rhubarb harvest

I've been scared of green living things
I have no way with them,
I don't understand them,
I cannot tame them.

The towering rhubarb stalks in our new yard
intimidated me.
But when I ventured there
one sunny morning
I came upon a lesser plant beneath
the seedy tower

Those small stalks had more
colour (the big ones bleached a woody green).
These younger folk blushed pink on their
fibrous canes, enjoyed a shady life under
the dappled umbrella green.
I spoke to them gently, brothers and sisters,
and cut them down,
every one, with my kitchen scissors.

I gathered those rosy limbs
bathed them, and chopped them into nuggets,
murmuring my thanks.

Last night the acid waft of rhubarb
wandered through our small new home,
coffee cake aroma blessed our domesticity.

Five bags of red-green summer—labeled,
compact, tame—lie sleeping in the freezer,
until heat and sugar set them free.

A house is a home

The house ticks time.
Fluid bodies move through it.

At night the house sleeps;
the bodies sleep.
Car headlights explode the black of the
still living room.
Hush, hush, back to sleep now.

House wakes at dawn and
puts its little lights on,
a warm living seed of a home
protecting its people, its cats.

House rumbles with laughter
when the man tells an
especially good joke to the woman.
(They think it's the refrigerator.)

House hums with
pleasure when the man
and the woman make love.

A honeymoon tale

So light and sweet, our honeymoon—
My luggage
forgotten
in the cab
to the airport.

I wore the same clothes
each day, washed my
socks at night, turned
panties inside out—felt happy,
content, complete.

You stayed at my side,
your hand warmed my flank—
endearments carried us weightless
through Manhattan. We have all
that we need, right now.

Papa H. was so angry when Hadley
forgot his suitcase at the station:
The horror of losing all that work.
And yet I like to think the loss lifted him.
Loss opens
a new page, splits a vein to bleed
from us the past.

I learned to walk my wedding
shoes from SoHo to Harlem,
Purple twinkling toes and new eyes
goggling the sights. No baggage
—just the clothes on our
backs and the timeless capers of
two people in love.

NYC Quartet

I. Guggenheim Pomme Poem
(After seeing the sculpture Pomona with Lowered Arms,
by Aristide Maillol, 1937, France)

Pomme
means apple in French
Apple, ample
inform you.
Your granny apple tits
contrast the soft bronze flesh
of your thigh.
I broke the rule,
crossed the line
to admire your spherical buttocks
and that roll of fat
just above your waist.

You were conceived
in love.
Love for women's
bodies, love of
heft, weight,
ordinary grandeur,
fertility.

No emaciated girl,
you are full-fledged

apple-of-my-eyed beauty.

II. Harlem Afternoon

Sitting in the skeleton Starbucks
at Lennox and 125th
I am an observer, a visitor.

I watch this theatre of the street
through glass, uninvited.

Malcolm X once walked here.
Hey
Detroit Red, Minister Shabazz,
I put you in a book—
I closed you off in definitive
academic argument.

I imagine your
leggy stride, your
long, earnest and bespectacled face
My words feel block-like,
uncouth,
before this fluid, black, poetry-in-motion.

III. MOMA Ennui

What's the big deal?
Just feel what you feel!
Like what you like, love what you love
Pure acceptance fits like a glove.

Our love is the safety
net they put under
scared naked people
jumping from burning buildings.
Our love is the web
under the trapeze walker
who teeters on the taut line.

Our love is elastic, firm, pliable
a pink blanket
pure energy
adjustable to all situations:
MOMA ennui
forgotten luggage
New York cold shoulders
moments of ecstasy.
Our love is so, so true.

IV. Thursday Bakery in SoHo

Jeweled Easter egg colours in
the glass case at Settepani's Pasticceria.
Light purple, candy pink,
mandarin orange, canary yellow.

Rows of pastries, pastel meringues,
glazed marzipan.
We sit in cannelli after glow,
coffee mouthed.
We sit sufficient unto
our selves, our love.
Our New York City walk
today was a dozen dazzling vignettes,
jewels hung on the knotted
silver cord of
our new marriage.
Five days young,
heart-forged,
poetry-steeped,
indomitable.

Death of the planet

Climate change is here.
Tornados, fires, and floods,
but we are safe
in our little world,
aren't we?

Nobody knocks on our
door. We like it that way.
Chicken in the pan,
potatoes roasting,
jazz on the stereo.

The only society we
seek is humming bees and
birds outside our window.
At night in our garden
we breathe flowers.

But they say the bees are dying
Detroit is bankrupt
Fires ravage California
Violence tears through Egypt
Let's turn off the TV.

Soon the bees
will all be dead.
(No more honey for
your coffee, my love.)
The fires are coming
nearer. We burrow deeper
into this domestic cocoon.
But our love cannot save us
from the death of this planet.

Paper sheets

We slept on a paper bed
white paper sheets and
blankets of crinkling yellow foolscap
fibrous mattress flat as a book
you write me into life
as I write you
lines legible only to us

The sex life of a middle-aged woman

Mrs. Dalloway climbs the tower stair
and makes her narrow bed.
A little younger than I,
Clarissa "had just broken into her 52nd year."
Married yet alone,
she is a brittle leaf.

I get into our big white-sheeted bed
turning on and off like a flesh furnace
burning up, soaking the linen
then freezing, pulling blankets to my chin

Your Reiki hands heat my root,
stir desire. I will not easily give up
this life Magog granted me
this pull of the confused womb
this sensitive nipple
this swelling clitoris

Pull me toward you
you are hard again.
Our puckered, lined,
beautiful bodies
roll together
Let's rock the bed
let's love

Let hags and crones
watch over us and shriek
with laughter

Dry egg
Seed not needed
Blood going, going, gone.
And yet this erotic river flows
thick, unbridled.

Mrs. Dalloway pulls a
thin sheet around her in
her coffin-like bed in
the lonely tower.
Joyfully, we pull
each other close,
bodies stuck with sweat,
and rock the big bed
once more.

V. Birth of the Uncool

The birth of the warrior is like the first growth of a reindeer's horns. At first, the horns are very soft and almost rubbery, and they have little hairs growing on them. They are not yet horns, as such: they are just sloppy growths with blood inside.

—Chögyam Trungpa, *Shambhala: The Sacred Path of the Warrior*

Aubade to the body

I wake this morning and
discover that I am still in my home,
this body.

My slender ankles rotate
without complaint,
my throat is clear,
my skin exhales
her earthy odours.

My belly, relaxed,
sags onto dark
red sheets, my strong legs
sprawl in a great Z.

My breath comes easy,
My blood thuds at the
root chakra,
pulsing her steady
rhythm, pa-dum,
pa-dum, pa-dum.

Dependable body,
wild mind,
we need a tight yet
flexible harness on the
broken path to
old age, sickness and death.

Elegy

Your child hungered for many milks.
Your inside child, that is, keen for death.
You sucked a multitude of poisoned breasts,
holding fast to those teats with fierce,
chapped hands. So now, after feeding
long and hard, death came like darling sleep.
You are set free.

Last cry

"A crowd flowed over London Bridge, so many,
I had not thought death had undone so many.
Sighs, short and infrequent, were exhaled,
And each man fixed his eyes before his feet."
—T.S. Eliot, "The Waste Land"

In this unreal city,
each walking dead man
fixes his eyes on his
cell phone.

The hyacinth girl
runs ragged on London
Bridge and threatens to throw
herself off—her red dress
a flag ignored by texters,
mutants.

Screens are
sucking you away! My tribe
is undone!
If you don't attend to Life,
I swear I'll jump!

So she jumps into the muddy
Thames, a vermilion swirl unnoticed.
She is not seen again until her

bloated naked body appears on the
banks of the Isle of Dogs on Sunday morning,
discovered by a Rotherhithe fisherman
who, feeling his loins stir at the sight,
pulls out his iPhone, points and clicks.

Hope shimmers

A string of coloured winking lights
wrap around a splintered
fence circling a shabby
house, but it's not Christmas—
not even close.

I am reminded of Blanche's
coloured lights in Streetcar—
she loved those shimmerings
to beat the band.
Poverty tinted warm with amber,
wrinkles diffused into rosy red,
despair sprouting into green.
Why not call it hope rather than delusion?
We all depend on the kindness of strangers.
I trust you not to kill me, after all.

This bracelet of lights
tremors bright hope for
world peace (as 39 Kenyans
are murdered, 78 Christians
explode) and we shimmer
in spite of it all.

Fist

A fist is a battle hand,
a tight weapon, closed for
business; no more words.

Fisticuffs—blunt fists cuffing blunt heads
in the alley back of the tavern

I have seen a fist penetrate glass
and the thousand drops of blood that
sprang like red dew on a white leaf.

Your raised fist cries
Power to the people!

Then noun became verb—let me fist you—
which seems a violent way to love.

How little I know of other people's lives.
Imagination can clench like a fist;
the fist a rampart to compassion.

Leo

Leo, seamed and smoky, in his green studio
pounds out the prostheses that go into mouths

Leo bends over the work table,
his cigar-like fingers finishing the fine,
small work of the denturist, modeling
pink acrylic to resemble human gums

The radio buzzes with yesteryear's top forty
Frankie Vallee, Tommy Dorsey.
Nicky boils the kettle for another cup of Nescafe
The plastic flowers quiver in the fan's breeze

Leo gazes out the back window
onto a parking lot instead of a yard
nurses his cup, sucks deep
on unfiltered Player's,
picks a fleck of tobacco from
his yellowing beard.

His smoky grey eyes
unfocus, go inward, as he
muses on the road not taken
many years ago.

Apocrypha

During her ninth August,
my mother carried a salt shaker
in the pocket of her sundress
every day.

Fat tomato clicks
off the aromatic vine
first bite warm spurt as tooth
tears skin, yellow seed on tongue,
second bite red meaty
mouthful, salty-sweet.

During his thirteenth winter,
my father called upstairs, voice cracking,
"Mother, where are my spectacles?"
"You don't need them, dear. Do your exercises"
and then my dad, sotto voce: "Damn that Dr. Bates!"

I like to imagine my mother and father as children
she the hedonist,
he the rebel.

Ego

Ego is lovely, her face boosted
by collagen. She wears a wig of human
hair and coloured contact lenses
turn her turbid windows to sick
turquoise.

She hawks self importance
like penny candy at the
front of the store, catching
the children before they
can get protein—you're
special, you're wonderful,
you're the best, ingested
with corn syrup
and hydrogenated palm
kernel oil,
            Addictive.

Cunning ego curls up
in your soul, like a python
seething gently. You might
be unaware of her presence
until you feel a constriction
around your neck

squeezing you
into small self
who gathers
bruises
and bounces
hotly
from
one
grievance
to
another
Give us a jab, anatta
to get us out of this fix.

Winston's dream

At one time or another
we all dream of the Golden Country,
archetype of paradise.

For Winston, rabbits crop the
pasture to short, springy turf.
Late sun gilds the ground.
Masses of leaves like a woman's hair
stir in the elms and the clear stream
stippled with fish, moves slowly.

He travels the path light footed.

Ancient place,
limpid place:
before spoilation,
prior to the serpent,
pre-addiction,
in advance of trauma,
anterior to Big Brother.

Where the ordinary
magnificence of an
arm flung toward
the sky promises
safety, promises
clean freedom.

Poetree

Trying will not make a poem
nor will loafing around it with tentative words
Fear doesn't help a poem
language gets skittish,
coy,
elusive.

What makes a poem is what makes
a tree. Seeded when you are
walking down the street
germ of a thought of a feeling
of a highflung hope

Seed burrows in mind and
puts out pea green shoots
those soft tendrils
make their way ahead

and soon the green fuse
is driving through you

you are falling down that emerald chute
where Stone, Livesay, and
Bishop fell before you

The lifewords are speaking
through you; your voice is
not your own but borrowed from
big Green.

Relax into it now
and the poem will grow
(you can prune it later)
trust the green good growth
of poetry.

Crackly and juicy

Throw down the robe of history—
stained, threadbare—here you stand

in your suit of skin looking so fine,
the patina of age blooming on your heavy

breasts, all the curves slackened now,
softened. What was a jutting hip

bone is now a fleshy cushion for
your husband's cheek. The past is

never past so the robe has to be
thrown down each day and your

birth day nakedness revealed
over and over so you can stay

fresh in this moment, noticing
every white hair blooming like

late summer cyclamen and
each laugh line crinkle at the

corner of your still bright eye
as you howl with laughter at

the loopy songs and wordplay
that embellish your marriage.

You are learning to sing and
belly breathe—pulling in oxygen to feed long lines of song.

You are at your most uncool now
age spotted, raggedy, not giving a shit,

saucy, insouciant, real,
crackly and juicy at once.

birth of the uncool

Back in the day,
We did not know cool or uncool
we knew running at the sun—blowing
huge wobbly soap bubbles and shrieking
when they burst, Pepper barking and jumping
at our bare calves burnished dark brown from
the everyday California sun. And running at the
sea on Stinson beach—wind whipped our hair
flying we whirled like dervishes and crashed
into the gelid salt-waves, swallowing water,
choking, laughing, choking.

Back in the day,
We learned how to print, read, do numbers
on the ten-foot blackboard in our playroom.
The walls were painted apricot because my
mother is, in her heart, an artist. The dolls sat
in miniature chairs watching us. The threadbare Indian
carpet was mottled with sun from the big windows. I
could pirouette around that big room with a piece of
chalk in my dirty hand and scat the vowels, a-i-e-o-u, a-i-e-o-u
whooooo—hooo

Back in the day
We looked for fire salamanders in the mud
over the big wall. The tow-headed neighbour boys
helped us, and there was no weirdness yet

and everything was Eden. Our cats stalked in
the big grass and nasturtiums piled up along
the edges of the yard. Mother was always doing
stuff in the house Father was out working or
studying. We had the yard, the playroom, the roof,
Berkeley's sun and rain, Le Conte schoolyard—these
were our world.

Back in the day
The rain poured and the worms came out. We
rescued each fat earthworm from certain
death, carefully moved them from the side-
walk and onto the green verge of Russell Street.
A morning's work squatting on pavement.
The cherry blossoms fell as hard as the rain some
days—pink air redolent of paradise.
We were promised nickel rides on the slowly
moving mechanical lion at the Co-op later,
if we behaved. It seems nobody
supervised children too much then. My
mother trusted we would be okay while
she bought bread, meat, coffee, rolling tobacco,
a quart of California Chablis.

* * *

When do you start to figure out that

it's cool to be cool? That cool is a way of
being that is not you—a way of playing
to the audience. First I am me, kooky,
gap-toothed, with tomboy bangs,
wearing funky corduroy jumpers sewn by my
mother, black tights and turtlenecks,
clunky shoes; eating what
is put on table,
singing to myself, flinging my body on
the carpet to play with the cats, roll
with the dog. I am unselfconscious in
my movements and free in my love for you,
and you, and you, and the universe.
I fling my arms around visiting friends and
grandmothers.

But then I start to see myself
out of the corner of my own brown eye:
Stupid to have bangs, first of all, when
the other girls in kindergarten park
their hair on either side of a line on
their skulls. Their clothes seem
different from my own.
Sally Butterfield wore a blouse with
pearly buttons, and I had never seen a
blouse before. The word was strange
in my ear. Blouse.

I started to see that my family was
awkward and silly and uncool, my mother wore
black tights under cut-off jean shorts:
ridiculous. My father had eczema on his
hands like a disease.
Before that, it was just "oh your poor
hands" as I kissed them rapturously all over,

wanting to heal them through my touch.
Now it was "yuck" and "don't touch me with those things!"

The worm turned: Birth of the cool had begun.
To be cool one has to care deeply what others
think—surveillance of the self.

* * *

On this day,
I gather up the tools for life drawing:
the kitchen timer and the conté, the board,
the paper. Undress and sit for me, darling, your
beautiful body, strong, aged, puckered,
built to last. I'll put you down on
paper in raw sienna, the folds and
mass, the sinew and the muscle.
Who cares if the kids see these
sketches tacked on our huge bulletin boards?
Who gives a shit what anybody
thinks of our uncool abandon?

Let's make an art room, not a
guest room in the new house.

On this day let's grab
our cameras and take pictures
of everything red and purple—
you do red; I'll do purple.
I will ask the barista if I can
take her picture (what a beautiful
plum sweater). The pile of
eggplants in Save-On Foods,
the surprise of a manhole
cover painted violet!

You are clicking reds:
the neon OPEN sign and
the red, red rose.

On this day
let's be uncool
let's wake up to this:
We are alive right now
and together. The world
bursts out each morning
to greet us—sickness and
death mingle among us like
party guests. We eat canapés
and small talk with them, but
let us dance only
with each other.

Works Cited

Anonymous. "Courage to Change: One Day at a Time." *Al-Anon II.* Virginia Beach, VA: Al-Anon Family Groups Inc., 1992. p.268. Print.

Eckhart, Meister. Web. http://www.brainyquote.com/quotes/m/ meister_eck149158.html. 27 Dec. 2013.

Eliot, T. S. "The Waste Land." *The Complete Poems and Plays, 1909-1950.* New York: Harcourt, Brace & World, Inc., 1992/1971. p. 39, l. 62-65. Print.

Miller, Alice. *Drama of the Gifted Child: The Search for the True Self.* Trans. Ruth Ward. New York: Basic Books, Inc., 1981. Print.

Milton, John. *Paradise Lost.* Book IX, l. 1053-5. 1667. Web. 27 Dec. 2013. Web. <http://knarf.english.upenn.edu/Milton/pl9.html>.

Rich, Adrienne. "Turning the Wheel." *A Wild Patience Has Taken Me This Far: Poems 1978-1981.* New York: W.W. Norton & Company, 1981. p. 54. Print.

Seuss, Dr. (aka Theodore Geisel). *I Had Trouble Getting to Solla Sellew.* New York, Random House, 1965. Print.

Trungpa, Chögyam. *Shambhala: The Sacred Path of the Warrior.* Boston: Shambhala Publications, 1984. p.36. Print.

Yeats, W. B. "A Dialogue of Self and Soul." *Selected Poems.* London: Phoenix, 2010. p.94. Print.

Acknowledgements

Thank you Andrea and the courageous team at Demeter Press who took a chance on me and gave me the opportunity to share my poetry. Thank you family, friends, and colleagues for your love and support for my creativity, shown in many ways. Thank you recovery programs and the people that work them and make them work. Thank you all poets. Thank you Academy of American Poets for Poem-A-Day, my inspiration. Thank you small presses everywhere—may you keep supporting artists even when money is scarce. Thank you Pema Chödrön, Peter Elbow, David Bayles, Ted Orland, and Julia Cameron for teaching me to let go, trust myself, and trust the process. But most of all, thank you Michael. In the cradle of our exquisite marriage, poetry, art, and magic are everyday phenomena. You are loving midwife to birth of the uncool.

Photo: Michael Carpenter

Madeline Walker is a writer and academic writing instructor at the School of Nursing at the University of Victoria. She holds a Ph.D. in American literature from the University of Victoria. Her first book, *The Trouble with Sauling Around: Conversion in Ethnic American Autobiography, 1965-2002,* was published in 2011. She has also published in *Room of One's Own* (now called *Room*), *University of Toronto Review,* the *Journal for Multi-Ethnic Literature of the United States,* and *English Studies in Canada.* Walker is interested in writing, writing pedagogy, art, and voice. Mother to three adult sons, she lives in Victoria, British Columbia, with her husband and two cats.